R. T. Ingalsbe

The teachers guide. A key to the International primary and business charts

R. T. Ingalsbe

The teachers guide. A key to the International primary and business charts

ISBN/EAN: 9783337712136

Printed in Europe, USA, Canada, Australia, Japan

Cover: Foto ©Lupo / pixelio.de

More available books at **www.hansebooks.com**

The Teachers Guide.

A KEY

—TO THE—

International Primary

—AND—

Business Charts.

F. T. INGALSBE, PUBLISHER,
744 Broadway, New York.

CONTENTS.

PREFACE.

I T was not originally designed to accompany the International Primary and Business Charts with a key, the author assuming that teachers, generally, were quite familiar with the subjects presented by the Charts, with the exception, perhaps, of Phonography, of which the rudiments only are here given,—a knowledge of which could be readily acquired from the Charts themselves.

But, since the publication and introduction of the Charts, the author has been repeatedly and earnestly solicited by teachers and school boards, to furnish them with a "Teachers Guide." In compliance with these solicitations, and with special regard to the wants and wishes of those whose experience in teaching has been quite limited, this volume has been prepared.

It is not designed to be a "complete guide" to the teaching of the subjects upon which it treats ; but rather to furnish such hints and suggestions as may lead to originality of method on the part of the teacher, "for no teacher should be a servile imitator or exact copyist." That it may serve to accomplish this result, and so far commend itself to the kindly consideration of teachers, is the sincere desire of the

AUTHOR.

To the Teacher.

NEARLY every teacher in the land will agree with us in the assertion, that, of all places where youth assemble either for pleasure or profit, the school room should be made the most attractive. The necessary means are just the same as those required to beautify private residences, with the addition of a live teacher, improved methods, text-books and apparatus; some of which are indispensable to a good school. Children will go where they are attracted; and is it not highly essential for their own interests and the interests of the school, that they be attracted towards the school room? This law of mind cannot be disregarded with impunity, and, indeed, everywhere else save in the school room it seems to be well observed—even the saloon keeper seems to understand well that to entice the youth into his place he must adorn it with elegant mirrors, showy engravings, and costly fixings generally. Is it any wonder that children dislike the school room—that study is often irksome to them, or that they are enticed into the saloon, and other places of like character,—places whose associations are well calculated to foster ignorance and vice? Intelligence and virtue must be made attractive or children will grow up ignorant and vicious. Why is it that this principle upon which success in business so much depends, is so sadly neglected in the school room,—the very place, where, of all others, its highest observance is demanded? Why is it that teachers are consigned to school houses with bare walls, uncarpeted floors,—without apparatus of any kind—and other like conditions, begetting indifference or perfect apathy on the part of the scholars, and yet expected to "teach a good school?" Such a state of things is very unfortunate for those earnest and energetic teachers, who wish to perform their duties fully and pleasantly, and who are thankful for any improvement in means and methods;—very unfortunate also for their schools. A grave responsibility rests somewhere that our schools are not better furnished, at least, with those requisites indispensable to a good school. Are the teachers themselves at fault? Or are School Boards mammoth "stumbling blocks" in the way of "attractive education?"

In the introduction of the International Primary and Business Charts, School Boards have generally urged as their only objection that "our teachers will not use them. If we could be assured that they would be faithfully used we would most gladly furnish our schools with them," etc., etc. I unhesitatingly express the conviction that School Boards, generally, are more willing to keep pace with the "advancing tide of intelligence" than they have had the credit of being;—but they must

be assured that what they do will not be in vain. It
must be confessed that they have not *always* received
this assurance. The fault lies, in part, with a class of in-
efficient teachers, (fortunately their numbers are rapidly
diminishing,) " who think their business dull work and
regret the necessity that compels them to continue in
it, who undertook it only to make a little money and
intend to leave it as soon as they can," and hence, feel-
ing no special interest in their vocation, neglect to examine the claims, or test the practical value of any apparatus furnished their schools ; and, in part, in the fact
that much of our school apparatus, although presenting
subjects of great importance *per se,* is attended by so
many disadvantages in its practical application, that its
use is either never undertaken or upon trial found to be
impracticable and soon discontinued. The dishearten-
ing effect of this result upon School Boards, has led
them to hesitate about supplying their schools with
needed apparatus for fear, as has been before observed,
"our teachers will not use it." Teachers should, therefore, in justice, at least, to their School Boards, do all in
their power to encourage their efforts in this direction,
by carefully examining, and thoroughly testing, the
practical value of whatever apparatus their schools may
be supplied with.

The series of Charts you are now required to use in
your school, is designed, first, to furnish for the younger
pupils, an Object Lesson in the Alphabet, Words, Reading, Orthography, and the Numerical Tables ; believing

that the best method of acquiring the elements of knowledge is through the medium of *visible objects*, and that their size, form, color, etc., all help to fix the attention and awaken an interest which, by the old method, it is generally quite difficult to arouse ; and, secondly, to furnish for the older pupils, in addition to Orthography, and the Numerical Tables above named, Phonography, and an elementary course of instruction in the science of doing business, consisting of the more practical part of what is taught in our Commercial Colleges, viz :—Business Forms ; Rules for Interest, Partial Payments, and Bank Discount; Letter Writing; and Book-Keeping ; thus affording an opportunity to obtain the most essential part of a Business Education, the value of which, in all the affairs of life, can scarcely be estimated.

The arrangement and methods of teaching these Charts, here presented, are not the result of untried theories, but, are based upon a plan of teaching which the author has tried and found useful, and hence they are recommended to teachers with confidence that every feature of them can be used to good advantage in the school room ; especially is this the case with the Book-Keeping Forms, which have been expressly adapted to the limited qualifications of teachers, generally, in this branch of study. The careful reading of the Book-Keeping instructions, it is believed, will be sufficient to satisfy the teacher who has previously paid but little attention to this subject, that it is easily within his reach to realize the most sanguine expectations of the author. From the difficulties heretofore attending its introduction as a regular study in our common schools, this subject has failed to receive that attention its importance demands. By these means, it is hoped, this difficulty may be entirely removed, and, thus, " that knowledge which all need and must have," whatever may be their occupation, may be no longer neglected.

The Multiplication Charts, also, will prove most efficient aids for the purpose intended. Experience has proved that, in schools where these Charts have been used by *live* teachers, even in one term, nearly or quite every pupil may thoroughly commit these tables to memory. "And, again, time spent in this way is often beneficial in other respects. It is found to be a pleasant and salutary diversion from book study, and tends to soothe the restless ones, who have become tired from long sitting." Every school should be supplied with more of such exercises.

The copying of the Business Forms will also be found a very advantageous exercise for the class organized for this purpose ; not only will it prove the best method of learning these forms, but as an exercise in Penmanship and Spelling, its value cannot be easily overrated. Again, the skillful teacher may arrange for this exercise at that hour of the day when the pupils are generally most restless, and hence most mischievous, and thus turn it to good account in securing order and industry in his school.

We have endeavored to use plain, simple language, believing that "when a new idea, or rule, is given to a pupil, it should be exposed to his gaze as much as possible by stripping it bare of all word covering, or forms of expression not perfectly transparent to him."

Other special features of these Charts are deserving of notice in this connection, but, since they have been sufficiently considered in the body of this work, it is not thought necessary to refer to them here. It is hoped enough has already been said to awaken an intelligent desire on the part of the teacher that will lead to their faithful and judicious use in his school. Such a result will be a rich reward to the

                                                    AUTHOR.

Teaching.

By Prof. A. S. WELCH, Ex-President Mich. Normal School.

PROMINENT educators of the West are aware that a radical change is taking place in the methods of Primary Education. In our best schools, there is a growing conviction that the old routine of early studies and old modes of teaching are out of harmony with the wants and instincts of childhood.

Many parents are beginning to inquire why it is that their little ones, though kept faithfully at school most of the year, make no satisfactory intellectual progress; and thinking men everywhere, who have this subject at heart, are perceiving the *worthlessness* of a system under which the precious years of life have been so often worse than wasted. It is conceded by the most experienced teachers, that the method originated in Switzerland by Pestalozzi, furnishes a complete remedy for these long standing evils. This method, modified to suit varying circumstances, now prevails in the schools of Germany and England, and is fast being adapted into the better class of primary schools of our country.

The Pestalozzian system differs from the old routine in several vital particulars. It recognizes the fact that the faculties of the child follow an invariable order of evolution, and it seeks to cultivate each faculty during the period of its growth, by supplying its appropriate food. It calls the pupil's attention to such *objects* as will gratify a natural curiosity, and thus makes the acquisition of knowledge a source of perpetual pleasure.

It gives a quickness and accuracy to the eye and ear; disciplines the perceptive powers whose activity is natural to early life; renders the pupil familiar with those objects which are most closely related to his future happiness; developes in him a love of the beautiful, and makes even his amusements contribute to his education. Finally, while it lays the foundation of *genuine culture*, in habits of close observation, it imparts that kind of knowledge which is of greatest worth in practical life. The officers of the Michigan Normal School, impressed with these facts, have, during the past few years, drilled its pupils in the new method, so far as was possible, without infringing upon the usual studies laid down in the catalogue. The Board of Education is now convinced that the time has come, when the school can render no greater service to the State, than to so modify its

(2)

course of study that all pupils may receive thorough instruction and practice in the Pestalozzian System of Primary Teaching.

Practical Education.

AVING become a practical people, discarding old notions and theories, it now becomes us to look to the training of those who are to follow us in the life battle that is opening upon us with such wonderful promise. They must be trained directly for the exercises of the age and times, and he who can best prepare and direct men and boys in the practical concerns of life, fitting them in the shortest time, and in the best manner, for successful, useful men, is the greatest benefactor. Not more than one-third of our young men, at the age of twenty-one, are qualified to meet with success in the business world, and it is to be greatly regretted that practical education, so essential to success, has been so much neglected. The training of our boys at the common school and academy has always been *theoretical*, and not sufficiently *practical and useful*. The result is that thousands of our young men, to-day, are *nobodies*, who might have been men of influence; and many others are engaged in pursuits that they heartily dislike, and in which they will never excel, simply because they have not confidence in themselves to make a change. There are also middle-aged men who have followed so long in the same old, beaten path of their ancestors, that their ambition has become blasted, and it requires the teaching of some leading spirit to arouse them from their lethargy, and bring out their talents and energies. Then, there are fathers by the score, who show no more judgment in the management of their sons than their horses, forgetting that the boy must sometime be the man, and that he can only rise to distinction and be independent, by being educated as *common sense* dictates, *in the school of practice.*

REV. MATHEW E. KING.

In this day and age, amid the light of the Nineteenth Century, it is beginning to be understood that to *succeed*, become eminent, or a leader in his business or profession, a man *must be practically educated.* The importance of educating our young men directly for active, useful life, has long been conceded by all true Americans. Our country was never so in need of practical, useful men as now, and it is time that this matter be more fully understood and discussed, and our schools and colleges be made to understand that cumbersome, impractical learning is at a discount, and practical education above par. The days of theory and old fogyism either in *teaching* or acquiring an education are passed. The teacher who expects to succeed in training the minds of the youth of America and is satisfied with the old beaten track of the theorist, will find that the present has left him far behind the age, his vocation gone, and himself left with his unpractical methods and views to seek some other way in which to gain a livelihood. The age demands that the education of young men and women be *practical,* and *thoroughly* so. In this fact may be seen the *reason* why so many of our schools fail in the education of the young. *They are not practical.*

N. Y. Tribune.

A Counting-house education will be of advantage to every man whatever his future occupation may be. To the farmers, it will teach business habits and attention to accounts, which will give them increased interest and success in their business.

To the mechanic it will teach order, system, management, the practical value of book-keeping, and remedy many of their deficiencies. To the professional man, it will afford a clearer insight into the operation of business affairs, and give him facilities in obtaining practice.

Freedley's Treatise on Business.

In a free country like ours, where so much work is to be done, no one need be idle, hungry or disreputable, who is able to work. We say, then, parents, give your boys a good *business education,* if you would insure their *success in life* and guard them against *vice* and *degradation.*

Mann.

Personal Accounts.

THINK every young man should begin forthwith to keep debit and credit with himself and with the world. If every man would resolve to know just where all the money that passes through his hands goes to, and would keep that account carefully, I venture to say there would be economies in his next year's account that were overlooked in the past. I hope these (Business) Colleges are destined to teach us method and order in our business, and in our industry. There are 500,000 farmers, probably, in the State of New York to-day, who, if you were to ask each of them how much per bushel his corn had cost him to grow for the last twenty years, I doubt if fifty of the 500,000 could tell you. And this is but one instance out of ten thousand. Now, every grower of agricultural products should inquire and ascertain, year after year, "What does this cost me? What does it bring me? Am I growing wheat at a profit, corn at a profit, and grass at a profit? Which among my products are profitable to me? On which do I realize a loss?" All business should be done with that constant regard to method;

but how seldom do we find this or anything-like it ? I venture to say that the young man who has commenced to keep an account of his time, to charge himself with wasted hours, with neglected opportunities, and with squandered means, will find himself very soon resolving on wholesome retrenchments and reforms.

I lay this down as a general rule, that any young man who, at the close of his first year of responsible, independent life has saved something and knows where to find it, will go on to competence ; whereas, the young man who, at the close of his first year has made nothing and has saved nothing—I do not say in money, but who has made himself no better off—will almost certainly die a poor man, and, if he lives in this city, he will probably be buried at the public cost.

HORACE GREELEY.

Primary Schools.

From "The Teacher's Assistant," by Charles Northend, A. M.; a Work of Great Merit, Published by A. S. Barnes and Burr, New York.

WE may differ somewhat in our estimates of these schools. In my opinion, they have never been properly appreciated nor suitably cared for. Lying as they do at the very foundation of a system of education, they are too often regarded as unimportant, though unavoidable, appendages to our common school system. Teachers of moderate attainments and without experience are often employed in them, merely because their services can be secured at a lower rate of compensation. But, in reality, these schools are of the first consideration, and they should receive the services and influence of the best of teachers. As it is in them that the young receive their earliest school impressions, it must be readily seen that it would be no easy matter to over-estimate their true importance. * * *

We well know that the instructions and influences to which we were exposed in early childhood, were those

which most strongly and indelibly impressed themselves upon our minds and characters. How many
lessons which we then learned, how many sights
which we then saw, how many impressions which we
then received, seem closely inwoven into our very na-
tures, and to be fresh and forceful in our memories,
while many of the lessons and scenes and incidents of a
later period are either wholly forgotten, or but dimly
and imperfectly remembered. How many there are
who pass through life constantly suffering from the influences of the exaggerated and fictitious stories, and
representations, to which they listened in childhood's
tender years,—influences which maturer years and riper
judgment cannot entirely eradicate, though they may
bring a sort of conviction of their falsity ! *   *   *

How many, during the first few years of their exist-
ence, have formed and fostered those uncharitable feel-
ings, and those distorted and unseemly habits, which
have tended to darken and embitter the whole current
of subsequent life !

In view of considerations like these, how essential is
it that special care and attention be devoted to the
early training of the young. *   *   * A distinguished
statesman once said, " Let me make the songs for the
youth, and I care not who make the laws." With far
more truth one might say, " Let me have the control
of the young during the first four years of their school
life, and I care not who has their subsequent management." *   *   *

(3)

How desirable, then, that these early lessons and influences should be of the right kind, and imparted in the right way. The mind of a child may be easily turned from a correct course by ill-judged and unwise plans, or by the chilling effects of neglect, on the part of those under whose care they pass their early years,—and some trivial circumstance, or some apparently insignificant cause, bearing upon the youthful mind, may give a change or tinge to the whole future life.

It would seem that parents acted less wisely in relation to this subject than in any other concern.   *   *

The farmer who has a colt to be trained, does not manifest indifference as to whom the task shall be committed; nor does he hazard injury and loss by trusting the work to incompetent hands, with a view to saving a few dollars and cents; for he well knows that much of the animal's value and usefulness will depend upon the manner in which he is " broken " to work and travel ;— and yet how passing strange is it that parents are often less wise and less interested in relation to the moulding and training of the immortal minds of their offspring, and that, for a trifling pecuniary saving, they will risk the happiness and usefulness of those whom God has intrusted to their charge !

Those employed to teach in our primary schools should not only be well qualified in a literary point of view, but they should abound in every lovely and desirable trait of character. Decided, kind, affectionate, pleasant and active, all their movements, actions and expressions should be such as may be safely and profitably imitated. The teacher of a primary school should be a pattern of every good,—a model worthy of the closest imitation.

George B. Emerson, Esq., a distinguished educator, in speaking of a recent visit to schools in Germany, thus strongly and beautifully testifies to the importance of elementary schools, and at the same time gives some valuable hints on teaching the alphabet: "The most striking and beautiful lesson I heard in Germany was in Dresden, conducted by a man of very high qualifications. It was a lesson in teaching the alphabet. Young ladies and young gentlemen are very apt to think, ' What a drudgery this is! only think, that, with my qualifications, I should be content to teach the beggarly elements! What a position! O, that I could be in a sphere fitter for my capacities!' That is a great fundamental mistake which leads any teacher to utter such words. *There is no lesson ever taught in any school so important as the alphabet.* Teaching our crabbed, English language, is the hardest thing in the world. Our language is the hardest one to read, from the fact that there is not the most remote connection between the words used and the sounds expected. *There cannot be a higher office than that of giving the very elements of instruction.*

" What was very striking, in the school at Dresden, was, that the teacher had a class of about forty boys, all nearly of the same age, and none of them less than seven years old, coming for the first time to learn the alphabet. Those sensible people, who wish to make as much as possible of their scholars, do not allow their children to be taught the alphabet before they are seven years old. The admirable teacher of these boys began by drawing a fish, and asking the boys to tell what it was. Some said it was a fish, some that it was a picture of a fish; but some that it had no color, and therefore was not a *picture*, but something the teacher drew. So they arrived, after a series of questions, at the conclusion that it was a *drawing* of a fish; not a picture, because that would have color; and not a fish, because that would have life. Then all the class were called on to say, together, 'That is a drawing of a fish.' As that would form a good sentence, they were required to repeat it till they could utter it as well as possible, giving every articulate sound clearly. Then he would ask each one to read the sentence. Then, from a set of large blocks, he selected the letters to spell the word *fish*, and, having shown them to the class, he asked them to select the letters to spell it, then to go to their seats and draw the letters on their slates. Some would succeed well, and some would fail entirely; but to those that failed there was no reproof, though to those that succeeded words of encouragement were given.

" In about ten minutes he called on the boys again, and inquired, ' What is a fish ?' and put several questions to lead them to think about a fish, and would converse with them about the facts in its natural history ;

and at each conclusion he would make them express their conclusions as well as their organs could utter it. That was the striking thing,—the lesson in making sentences, in speaking good German, and. in pronouncing correctly.

The first thing to be noticed here is the fact that a gentleman of the highest intelligence, possessed of all knowledge, a beautiful knowledge of natural history, did not think himself degraded in the least degree by teaching the alphabet. Another thing to be noticed was, that those things which, in the old-fashioned schools, were considered unsuitable, they were encouraged to do,—that is, to make pictures. Another thing that was very noticeable, was the thoroughness with which the languages were taught in the gymnasia. The master would have forty boys of just the same age and the same attainments. The little which the teacher attempted to teach at one time was a striking feature of the instruction. A single short sentence of three words was given ; but in regard to them he led them to observe everything, and reviewed everything they had become familiar with, and they were kept familiar with it by continual repetition. After they had learned a single sentence, they were to use that in making other sentences. The degree of thoroughness with which this instruction was given almost transcends belief."

I trust the extract just given   *   *   *   will tend to elevate, in your mind, the primary school.   *   *   *   It is very desirable that you should possess right views,

and a proper estimate of its true importance in the
great system of popular education. If you clearly understand the subject, you may do much for the dissemi-
nation of correct sentiments.

Phonography.

By Prof. C. A. Walworth.

UNSON'S System of Phonography is now recognized as the best modern system of short-hand writing. It is the most *efficient*, the most *simple*, and the most *systematic*. While retaining all the general and most valuable features of previous methods, it has introduced important improvements, which have received unanimous commendation from unprejudiced, competent judges throughout this country, and even in England. Of leading systems of Phonography, it is the most modern, and its author has had more practical experience in *verbatim* reporting than any of his predecessors. Its great simplicity, as well as efficiency, makes it now possible for the public to realize the high anticipations long held of the valuable uses to which short-hand might be applied in the daily affairs of life. This system has recently been officially adopted by the Board of Public Instruction, after thorough comparison with other methods, and introduced, as a regular study, in the College of the City of New York.

There is, evidently, at the present time, a wide-spread and increasing appreciation of the utility of Phonography, and a corresponding *demand* for qualification in it.

Phonographers are being regularly employed by all our principal courts, and lawyers do not like to examine a witness in any case without the aid of a short-hand writer. Many attorneys, indeed, are making it a uniform practice to compose their *briefs* by dictating to a short-hand writer ; and leading law firms are employing one or more phonographic clerks in their offices by the year, at regular salaries. Every law student should learn this art, for he will find it invaluable for his personal use in a still greater variety of ways in the practice of his profession.

Literary men, editors, authors, etc., are employing phonographic amanuenses with great advantage. Editors dictate their editorials, and authors compose whole books, with great saving of time and labor, by simply employing an efficient phonographer. Every man who has a *large and important correspondence* should employ a short-hand dictation and corresponding clerk, and thus save himself the main labor, *while retaining the benefit of responding in his own words, and with promptness*, to all letters. This latter use of the art is impelling many of our prominent business men to seek its advantages, and vastly many more will do so as soon as they see how easily it is accomplished.

The great advantages of employing phonographic corresponding clerks, or secretaries, as above indicated, deserve more attention. *In no other way* can every man who is burthened with a large correspondence, which should not be neglected, respond to its duties *promptly*, *fully*, and *in his own language*, without unnecessarily taking valuable time, doubtless needed for other purposes. In this way, the work of *a day* can be done in *an hour*, and, with the aid of that other modern invention, the copying-press, the principal always has at hand evidence of the faithfulness of his amanuenses. This plan has already been adopted by many leading professional and public men, and by heads of large business establishments, especially of INSURANCE COMPANIES, Banks, etc. Mr. James Parton, the eminent author, has referred to this subject in a newspaper article, entitled, " What floored Mr. Colfax," showing that the Vice President's sudden prostration a year ago, in the Senate, was caused by not employing such assistance. Although the best phonographic law reporting in the world is done in this city, under the encouragement of official appointment of court stenographers, with yearly salaries, it will surprise many to learn that the English have been more enterprising than we in the employment of the art for business purposes. Several of the leading railways running out of London have, for more than five years past, required their clerks, at all the stations, to be qualified in phonography, and they find its

(4)

general use by them to be of great advantage in their business.

All young persons who propose attending college or professional schools, where some of the instruction is given by lectures, should thoroughly qualify themselves in this art, so that they may be able to secure the full advantages of such lectures, besides deriving the other benefits the knowledge of phonography will be to them then and afterwards.

There is an increasing tendency on the part of young men, and ladies, also, to enter the journalistic profession, but how to specially educate themselves for it has been a puzzle. The profession, at this day, demands persons directly qualified for its duties, and some of the more intelligent and enterprising editors have suggested the establishment of a regular school of journalism. One difficulty seems to be that phonography is the only branch yet found that can be used towards this purpose. A practical command of this art, alone, is, at present, the best special preparation for getting a situation on the press. Charles Dickens, and other eminent English authors, began professional life as short-hand reporters, and, in this city, Theodore Tilton, Oliver Dyer, and other newspaper men, are additional instances.

Many persons learn Phonography with no intention of ever using it professionally, but simply for their own satisfaction, or private use. *The time is near at hand when it will be a regular study in schools generally.* One advantage of this subject is that it tends to make a person *perfect in pronunciation,* probably more so than any other branch. The study itself is very fascinating, instead of being dry and difficult, as many suppose. Amateurs use short-hand for keeping diaries, making memoranda, composing, copying, and for taking notes of speeches, etc.

Phonography, penmanship, and business correspondence, open a fine field for remunerative, light office work for ladies, besides being useful accomplishments for many other purposes. Those who will thoroughly qualify themselves in these subjects, can hardly fail of securing desirable positions.

It is a common but erroneous impression about Phonography, that it is simply the work of some ingenious mind, who has invented, entirely by himself, an alphabet of *brief signs,* which a learner, by long practice, and probably the addition of some arbitrary characters of his own devising, can use to write the language rapidly enough for reporting purposes. Now, this idea contains two serious errors: First, Phonography is the perfection of short-hand writing, which has existed and has accumulated the ingenuity of man in this direction for more than 1900 years. We have knowledge of a system, and a specimen of its alphabet by Tiro, of the date of fifty-five years before Christ, and even some information of previous methods, extending as far back as that of Pythagoras, who lived, B. C., 555. In England the first system appeared in 1588, and since that time others have been brought out every few years down to the invention of Phonography by Isaac Pitman, of Bath, England, in 1837. Like other inventions and discoveries, each later work has naturally derived advantages resulting from the experience of previous systems, and even Phonography, though radically different, because of its phonetic basis from preceding kinds of short-hand, contains the best features of the others, and represents, as thoroughly as any other branch of knowledge, the degree of perfection which ages of investigation and use produce. Phonography, from having the only correct basis, has superseded all other methods, but its present degree of perfection is specially due to the labors of several authors and the experience of hundreds of phonographic reporters. Persons, therefore, should not suppose that the best modern system of short-hand writing is of a *temporary character*, and liable to be displaced in a hurry, but that from its *age alone* it is entitled to rank with other school studies.

The second popular error is, that a person learning the art need not conform to it in every respect. With Munson's Phonography, however, which is a thorough-tested, harmonious, and practical system, even in its *minutest details*, and represents the perfection of Phonography as well as short-hand in general down to the present time, such an idea is a great misapprehension. On the contrary, the learner should conform to it in every particular, both while learning and in all his subsequent practice, for the more thorough and pains-taking he is in this regard, the more certain will be his success and satisfaction.

When the importance of Phonography is thus brought to the attention of individuals, the question is frequently asked : "Why has not this art been more successfully and generally learned already ?" coupled, perhaps, with the observation that they know of many persons who have studied it, but are not known to have received much practical benefit. The answer to this question is, that it has been from the want of an *efficient* system and *efficient* teaching. The earlier systems were inadequate, either from being only elementary, or unnecessarily complicated, or both, and there was scarcely any teaching done in a thorough and practical manner ; but this study was placed secondary to all others and received only meagre or irregular attention.

To the Teacher.

Description of the International Primary and Business Charts, and Methods of Teaching the Subjects Presented by Them.

— o —

The Alphabet Chart.

HIS Chart is arranged to present the Capital letter first,—made large, so that the class standing before the Chart may all see it distinctly ; then follows the small letter, and a combination of letters, or a word, in which the previous letter is an initial; and lastly, words having real objects in the school-room are selected. Thus, by associating the words with the objects which they represent, the child learns at the outset their true meaning and use, and it will not thereafter be satisfied with merely pronouncing them. The teacher is also enabled by asking appropriate questions, to excite not only a lively interest in the exercise, upon which success in teaching so much depends, but also to impart much valuable information.

The Object and Word Method Chart.

THIS CHART is arranged to present the object, or the picture of the object first; next, in each picture, two separate objects have been designated by the respective words naming each, for the purpose of testing the pupil's ability to select the word called for, and the words are printed near the picture in order that an intimate association may be formed between the picture, its name, and the word which stands for the name. Each word commences with a capital letter, and in the list of words each capital letter is given once or more,—arranged so as to break up the old routine of reciting the letters from A to Z. And, lastly, there is the expression of a thought in words, asking a question or stating some general truth respecting the object represented by the picture.

Teaching the Alphabet.

THERE ARE two methods of teaching the alphabet. The first commences with letters, and may be called

the A B C method. The second commences with
words, and may be called the Word method.

The A B C Method.

Should the teacher prefer the A B C method, the
Alphabet Chart may first be used, but the Object and
Word Chart may be used advantageously in connection
therewith, especially in the hunting exercise, to which
reference will hereafter be made. The teacher may select at the commencement, a few of those letters which
possess the most easily remembered forms, as O, X, and
S,—describe them, and point out their peculiarities and
resemblances, give their names, and ask questions about
them. "The capital and small letters should be taught
at the same time. Those letters which are alike will
be remembered from their resemblance, and those that
differ from contrast; and one class of letters will be
needed by pupils about as soon as the other."

The child must also be taught, at the very outset the
nature and object of each letter, or he will not take a
proper interest in the exercise; for this purpose the
teacher may say to the class:

Teacher.—"You see this letter. Now look at me.
You all know me when you see me. Now I wish you
to look at this letter, so that you will know it whenever
you see it. It stands for a *sound*. Listen, and hear me
give the sound."

"Having enunciated the sound, distinctly, several times, taking care to secure the attention of all, the teacher might ask if any one has ever heard the sound before. Some may remember it, as given among the elementary sounds of the language. If so, they are pleased to find that the lesson is connected with something learned before. If it is not recalled, give the vowel sounds promiscuously, requesting all to put up hands when they hear it.

TEACHER.—"Now all give the sound after me. Again. Again. That is what this letter says. When you read it you give the sound."

The teacher may next engage the class in a *general hunt*—using both charts for this purpose—for as many letters as they can find like those they have learned,— hunting for but one letter at a time. This search for the letters will be found very interesting and profitable, " and when the recitation has ended, the pupils will take their seats reluctantly, and wait impatiently till the time again arrives when they can have another game of ' hide and seek ' with letters."

The teacher may now make the letters of the lesson upon the black-board, directing the attention of the pupils to the manner in which they are made, as follows :

TEACHER.—" See me make this letter on the board. I begin here, and go around in this way. You may now come to the board and try to make it."

With a little help and encouragement from the teach-

(5)

er, all will succeed very well. They may repeat it two
or three times.

TEACHER.—" You may now go to your seats, and try
to make them on your slates."

" One of the advantages of using the slate and black-
board in teaching the alphabet, is, that the teacher can
furnish pleasant employment for the class when not engaged in reciting. Children are very fond of work of
this kind, and it will be found to greatly facilitate their
progress."

It is not designed that the teacher shall adhere to the
method here laid down, strictly, and at all times.
" Children are fond of variety, and it can hardly be
doubted that a teacher who varies his methods and
means of teaching, will cause his pupils to make more
progress than one who confines himself to a single
method, or to the same means, even though he may
choose the best."

The Word Method.

THIS METHOD of teaching the alphabet seems to be
the most natural. " Children use words in speaking,
and the transition seems natural from spoken to written
words, and then to the letters of which words are composed. If we commence with letters, there can be no
immediate connection between that knowledge of language which the pupil has, and that which he is ex-

pected to acquire. Besides, the Word Method follows the order in which written language was invented. Characters were first used for objects, next for words, and last for letters.

"It possesses more interest for children. A child cannot be made to take much interest in abstract, arbitrary forms like *a, b, c ;* while all children delight in talking about a *bird,* a *dog,* a *bell,* a *coach,* and consequently may be pleased to learn the words for such objects, and the letters composing such words. Teachers unconsciously show the truth of what is here said, when they tell their pupils that *a* stands for *apple, b* for *boy,* and *d* for *dog,* etc."

If the Word Method be adopted by the teacher, the Object and Word Chart should first be used. The lessons may at first embrace only the words which stand for the objects represented in the pictures. After having learned several of these words the pupil may be exercised upon words disconnected from pictures or objects, as in the A B C Chart. Only two or three words should be given the class at a lesson, and the shortest words, such as *man, car, dog,* etc., should be selected at the commencement, for the convenience of the pupil in drawing upon the black-board or slate.

The Chart having been placed before the class, the teacher may select a single object to begin with. Suppose it to be the picture of the dog:

TEACHER.—" You all see this picture. What is it ? is it a dog, or the picture of a dog ? When you see this

picture of what does it make you think ? Now here is
a word that makes me think of a dog. I wish you all
to look at this word, so that you will know it when you
see it again. When you see this picture, of what do you
think ? When I see this word, of what do I think ?
Then we will call this word dog. What is it ?" All
say dog.

The teacher may thus exercise the class upon not
more than two or three words at each lesson, then, re-
turning to the first word, request the class to point it
out to him, then the second, and the third. The words
may now be drawn upon the black-board—taking care
to show the class how each letter is made, and requiring
them to make it first upon the board, giving them the
necessary assistance and encouragement, and then upon
their slates, after resuming their seats. As soon as the
class have learned to distinguish readily the words, or
several of the words, in connection with the pictures,
they are prepared to analyze these words, and ascertain
the parts of which they are composed, or to learn their
letters. The words first selected for analysis should be
short, and, in analyzing them into letters, the same plan
may be pursued as that described when speaking of the
A B C method.

The Sounds of the Letters.

This Chart consists of two tables. The first is arranged to present a list of words containing a classifica-

tion of the sounds of the English language, together with the standard letter, or letters, used to represent each sound, thus : First, the vowel sounds,—expressing the letter for the sound heard in pronouncing its *name*, and indicating the other sounds represented by the *same* letter without repeating the letter, thus showing those sounds having no letter to represent them, but, for which, some *other* letter must be substituted. The table of consonants includes also those *elementary* sounds, which, having no character to represent them, are represented by the substitution of *two* letters, each, when standing alone, representing *other* and different sounds. The words selected are arranged in rhyming pairs, in order to make the concert exercise more easy and attractive ; and those words which, in their pronunciation, unmistakably give the consonant sounds of W and Y, have been selected for that purpose.

The table below comprises a partial list of letters representing other sounds than those assigned them in the first, or standard table. Letters so employed may be called substitutes for those they take the place of. Thus, in the word *any*, *a* represents the vowel sound heard in the word *egg*, and assigned to the letter *e ;* *a* is hence substituted for *e*. In the word *obey*, *e* represents the vowel sound heard in the word *ate*, and assigned to the letter *a*, etc. In the word *nor*, *o* represents the vowel sound heard in the word *all*, and assigned to the letter *a*. This sound is also often represented by the combination *au*, but it would, nevertheless, be incorrect if we were to adhere to the standard table of sound representatives. In the word *rude*, *u* represents the vowel sound heard in the word *do*, and assigned to the letter *o*. In the word *missed*, *d* represents the consonant sound heard in the word *it*, and assigned to the letter *t*. In the word *can*, *c* represents the consonant sound heard in the word *oak*, and assigned to the letter *k*. In the word *vicious*, *ci* represents the *single* consonant sound heard in the word *ash*, and assigned to the combination *sh*. And in the word *wax*, *x* represents the *two* consonant sounds heard in the word *oaks*, and assigned to *k*, and *s*, etc.

General Directions.

The teacher should drill the school in concert, at a regular time each day, in the elementary sounds of the language, using the standard table for this purpose, at first, in connection with the words in which the sounds are heard, and then separately, until all are well understood, and can be readily given when required. In every school there are some pupils who find it exceedingly difficult to articulate every sound readily and distinctly. Especial care should be taken that such pupils utter the sounds correctly. They should be required to utter them after the teacher, and carefully guided in placing their organs of speech in the proper position to do so.

The table of "Letters representing other Sounds than their Own," may be used very advantageously in the process of analyzing words into the elementary sounds of which they are composed. The method of doing this may be, substantially, the same as that given in the description of this table. The peculiar advantage of this plan arises from the necessity of knowing the sound before it can be determined whether the letter used to represent it is its standard representative or not. It must also be discovered that the letter is not the *real sound,* itself, but only the *picture* of the sound, the same as the representation of a house on paper is not the house itself, but only the picture of a house. This discovery having been made, it then becomes apparent that it is quite as consistent to represent a horse, indiscriminately, by the picture of a horse, cow, or any other picture, as to represent a sound by two, three, or a dozen pictures, or letters, entirely different in their appearance; which is a case of not unfrequent occurrence in the English system of orthography.

Thus, by using this table in connection with the one above, the incompleteness of our orthography, in having an insufficient number of characters to represent *all the sounds* of the language, and the inconsistency, or absurdity, of using those we have in the manner in which they are used, may be amply shown.

It is earnestly urged that the subject of orthography be paid that attention, in our primary and common schools, its importance demands; and it is confidently believed that the method here suggested will be found one of the best for general purposes. By using the black-board, the teacher may extend his illustrations indefinitely.

The Multiplication Tables.

THERE are, probably, few teachers of Primary Schools in the land, who will not agree with us, that there is no other subject of common school instruction, upon which the same amount of time has been spent, with such disproportionate results, as in the study of the Multiplication Tables. This arises, we apprehend, in part, from the nature of the subject itself, and, in part, from the defective methods by which it has been taught. These tables, consisting, as they do, of several hundred multiplications, appear to the mind as a vast collection of unrelated facts, each of which must be recollected independently, and each of which, therefore, is very easily forgotten. As presented on the Charts, this disadvantage is largely overcome by exhibiting, to the eye, a tangible object to which the idea can be attached. "The arrangement, color, size, and shape of the figures, all help to fix them, and their com-binations, firmly in the mind, the same as the use of the object in teaching any other subject."

(6)

Arrangement of the Multiplication Tables.

Each Multiplication Table is so arranged as to form a combined Multiplication, Addition, and Subtraction Table. This result is effected by placing two successive Multiplication Tables, (commencing with the twos,) on each chart, in the following manner: The products of the several multiplications in the first table are placed in the left margin of the chart, and the products of the several multiplications in the second table are placed in the right margin of the chart. The multiplicands, from 1 to 12, are arranged in a vertical column, upon a "key-board," which is designed to cover the printed matter in the body of the chart when the tables are in use; and the index figure, or multiplier, is centrally placed above the table to which it belongs.

Reading the Tables.

1st.—Multiplication Tables.

Commencing with the Table of Twos, the Multiplication Tables are read as follows: 2 (index figure) times 1 (key-board) are 2, (left margin); 2 (index figure) times 2 (key-board) are 4, (left margin), etc. The Threes are read thus : 3 (index figure) times 1 (key-board) are 3, (right margin) ; 3 (index figure) times 2 (key-board) are 6, (right margin), etc.

2d.—Addition Tables.

COMMENCING with the first figure in the left column, the Addition Tables are read from left to right, horizontally across the page, as follows: 2 (left column) and one (key-board) are 3, (right column); 4 (left column) and 2 (key-board) are 6, (right column), etc.

3d.—Subtraction Tables.

COMMENCING with the first figure in the " key-board," the Subtraction Tables are read from right to left, horizontally across the page, as follows: 1 (key-board) from 3 (right column) leaves 2, (left column); 2 (key-board) from 6 (right column) leaves 4, (left column), etc.

Recitation of the Tables.

FIRST METHOD.—The whole school should be drilled upon the tables in concert, at a regular time each half-day. The recitation should be " short and spirited," never continuing until the interest in it begins to abate. Commencing with the twos and threes, (the card having been placed upon the wall, and the " key-board " properly adjusted,) the teacher, with pointer in hand, will call attention to the object of the index figures (2 and 3) above the first and second tables, and, requiring the class to answer promptly, will proceed, rapidly, as follows :

TEACHER.—" 2 times 1 are how many ?   2 and 1 are how many ?   3 times 1 are how many ?   1 from 3 leaves how many ?   2 times 2 are how many ?   4 and 2 are how many ?   3 times 2 are how many ?   2 from 6 leaves how many ?" etc.

Proceed in this manner through the twos and threes, and from table to table, until all are thoroughly learned.   It would be well, however, to precede this method by the second, to which reference is made below.

It is not expected, nor desired, that the teacher will observe the same invariable order in his questions, as has been here observed ; but, on the contrary, the teacher who would succeed in keeping up a lively interest, must vary the order of his questions indefinitely. This method is possessed of numerous advantages, three or four of which, may be noticed in this connection :   First.—By reciting the Multiplication, Addition, and Subtraction Tables in combination, and thus changing rapidly from a table of one kind to a table of another kind, it commands the attention of the class as no other method can.   Second.—It cultivates quickness and accuracy. Third.—It affords a thorough test of the pupil's proficiency in memorizing the Multiplication Tables. Fourth.—It is a very valuable auxiliary when used in connection with the " Concert Method," of reciting these tables ; which, however valuable, is not complete in itself, and, when used alone, is subject to great abuse. These methods should, therefore, be used in conjunction with each other.

SECOND METHOD.—This method, pertaining exclusively to the recitation of the Multiplication Tables, is called the " Concert Method," and is supposed to be so generally known that an elucidation of it is not considsidered necessary in this place. It is very valuable for some purposes, when well conducted, and may be profitably used in connection with the method above described. Each recitation should be " short and spirited," consisting, after the first, of a review of the last table recited and one in advance. When the tables have all been recited in this manner, the class should begin back with the first table, and proceed as before.

NOTE.—The elemental ideas of Multiplication, Addition, and Subtraction, should be explained to those pupils who have no knowledge of them, by the use of the Numerical Frame, or, in the absence of that, the black-board will answer every purpose.

Business Forms.

THE Business Forms are designed to be copied into blank-books, prepared for that purpose, until the forms and their contents are indelibly fixed in the mind; as experience has shown this to be the best method of acquiring that *practical* knowledge of them which their *use* requires. The blanks required may correspond in size with the "copy-books" in general use, and the teacher should see that they are neatly and tastily prepared.

To render their use practicable, or desirable, the Forms have been enlarged, so that they can be copied without difficulty when placed upon the wall, since it is only in this way that they can be used to advantage in the school-room.

General Directions.

ALL scholars who can write may profitably engage in this exercise, and, since the arrangement of the Forms need not, necessarily, observe any particular order in the copy-book, to facilitate the exercise, and to accommodate all at their respective seats, different ones may be allowed to copy from different charts at the same time.

SPELLING.—The teacher should frequently visit the pupils while at their work, making such suggestions, respecting its style and character, as he may deem necessary. Especially should he see that all words are correctly spelled, and that the strictest attention is paid to punctuation, capitalization, neatness, and accuracy.

PENMANSHIP.—The teacher should also make such suggestions, concerning the position at the desk, the holding of the pen, etc., as may be necessary to a constant improvement in penmanship. The copying of these Forms will be found a most valuable exercise for this purpose. I am of the opinion that in no other way can practical business penmen be made so surely and so quickly, as in the copying of promiscuous reading matter, under the constant care of a good teacher of penmanship. For this reason this exercise may very properly occupy the writing hour.

BUSINESS FORMS.—The nature, object, and manner of using every business form should be explained to the pupils before they are allowed to copy it. After the promissory notes have been copied once or more, as the teacher may think best, the card may be turned over and the pupils required to fill up the Blank according to the different forms on the charts, or others that may be given by the teacher. The Blank Form will be found very serviceable, not only as a test of the pupils' proficiency in their work, but as affording a means whereby the knowledge already acquired may be practically applied, thus strengthening and making more permanent its impression upon the mind ; and, again, in actual business, the pupils will often be called upon to fill up blanks of various kinds, and they should have previous practice or they will not be able to do so when required. For this purpose the teacher may write blanks of other business papers upon the blackboard and require the pupils to fill them up correctly. Especially should they be practiced in filling blank orders, checks, drafts, receipts, etc.

The teacher should strive to give every lesson as practical a turn as possible. An excellent method of doing this is to require the class, after having had sufficient practice in copying, to prepare for him, as he may need to use them, the various business papers, on the supposition that they are required by him in his transactions with his customers ; or, what would be better still, the teacher could procure at a trifling cost, at any commercial college, several hundred dollars in bank bills of different denominations, and by this means he could institute transactions with his pupils, requiring all kinds of business papers ; thus, he could loan money and require a note, or pay borrowed money and call for a receipt, or be his pupils' banker and require them to check out their deposits, etc. Such practice would give the pupils *full command* of the knowledge so acquired, and it would not be easily forgotten.

Commercial Papers.

Promissory Notes.

A PROMISSORY NOTE is an unconditional written promise by one person to another, for the payment, at a specified time, of a certain sum of money. Promissory notes containing the word *bearer*, or *order*, may be bought and sold, or transferred from one to another. Notes so drawn are called Negotiable Notes. (See Chart). Notes that do not contain the word *bearer*, or *order*, cannot be transferred, and hence are called Non-Negotiable Notes ; thus, this note, (See Non-Negotiable Note,) containing a promise to E. W. Tryon, but not to *bearer*, or *order*, is good in Tryon's hands, but it is not negotiable,—it cannot be transferred to any other person.

A note containing the word *bearer* is transferable by delivery alone ; thus, in this note, (See Negotiable Note, without Indorsement,) the promise is to pay George

Mansfield, or *bearer*, and hence it is good in the hands of any person who may have it when due ; for the promise is to pay the *bearer*.

INDORSEMENTS.—But in this note, (See Negotiable Note, with Indorsement,) containing the word *order*, the promise is to pay George R. Whitmore, or *order*, hence it cannot be transferred by mere delivery, but Whitmore must order it paid to some one else before the transfer can be made. The simple writing of his name across the *back of the note*, (See Indorsements,) is understood to be his order for its payment. The writing of one's name across the back of a note is called an *indorsement*, and the writer is called the *indorser*.

SPECIAL INDORSEMENT.—If the indorser writes over his signature the words, "Pay to (name) or order," he thus gives special, or full directions, as to whom, or whose order it shall be paid, and hence it is called a *special*, or *full indorsement*. If the directions are to "Pay to John Curtis, or order," as at No. 2, Curtis is made the *payee*; but, if he wishes to dispose of the note, he must also indorse it, for it is made payable to him, or his *order*, and his indorsement is his order to pay it to another. If Curtis, in transferring the note, makes a special indorsement, then, before it can be again transferred it must receive a *third* indorsement. In like manner indorsements may be, and frequently are made until the back of the note is filled, and a paper is attached to it for the purpose of receiving other indorsements.

BLANK INDORSEMENT.—If the indorser writes only his signature across the back of the note, leaving the space above it blank, as at No. 1, and the note open to circulation without limitation, it is called an *open*, or *blank indorsement*. By such an indorsement the note becomes the same as a note drawn payable to *bearer*, and *may* pass through the hands of A, B, C, or any number of persons without further indorsement. But any subsequent holder, as C for instance, has the right, if he pleases, to make the indorsement special, by writing in the blank space above the indorser's signature, the words, " Pay to (name) or order," as at No. 2. It must *now* be indorsed by the person to whom it is made payable before it can be again transferred. The indorser of a note guarantees its payment, and is liable to the holder on due notice of its non-payment by the maker. If the maker of a note fails to pay it when due, the first indorser becomes responsible for its payment; should both of these fail to make payment, then the second indorser becomes responsible, and so on.

QUALIFIED INDORSEMENT.—But if any indorser wishes to avoid all responsibility, he may do so by writing over his signature the words, " without recourse," as in No. 3, which is called a *qualified indorsement*. But these words do not prevent its being made a blank or special indorsement the same as if they had not been used. (See No. 3.)

OTHER INDORSEMENTS are sometimes made for special,

or private purposes, as at Nos. 4, 5, 6 and 7 ; but as
there can be no difficulty in understanding them at a
glance, it is not considered necessary to dwell upon them
here.

Bank Notes.

BANK NOTES, usually called bank bills, are promissory notes, "issued by a banking company, signed by
the president, and countersigned by the cashier, and
payable to the bearer in gold or silver, or in whatever
is made by the laws of the state or country a legal tender, on presentation at the bank and demand of payment. Bank Notes are, of course, negotiable, being
made payable to *the bearer*; and they are usually secured by a deposit of State Stocks, or United States
Stocks."

SPECIAL DIRECTIONS.—The class should be shown a
Bank Bill, and their attention called particularly to the
fact, that it is drawn like any other promissory note,
payable to *bearer*.

Certificates of Deposit.

PERSONS who deposit money in a bank, are, at their
request, furnished by the bank with a writing acknowl-

edging the receipt of the money, and promising to pay it to the order of the depositor at a given time, or on the return of the writing properly indorsed, with or without interest, as specified in the writing. Such a writing is called a Certificate of Deposit; but it is in reality a promissory note, given by the bank to the depositor, for *value* received. (See Certificate of Deposit.) When money is deposited in a bank with the expectation that it will not be drawn out in the ordinary course of business, the depositor may very properly require the bank to give him a certificate of deposit, as evidence of its indebtedness.

Judgment Notes.

A JUDGMENT Note is like any other promissory note, with the exception that it has attached to it a power of attorney, authorizing the holder to enter up judgment thereon if not paid when due.

Property Notes.

A NOTE payable in *property* specified is called a Property Note, but is sometimes considered as an *agreement* merely. If not paid when due, the payee has the right to demand the *money*, and may claim damages for the non-fulfillment of the promise.

Due Bills.

A WRITTEN acknowledgment that a certain sum of money, or a specified amount of goods, or property, is due to a party therein named, or to his order, or to the bearer, is called a Due Bill. "Due Bills are either promissory, or property notes, though less formal than notes usually are. Whether negotiable or not depends upon the circumstances just enumerated."

Orders.

A WRITING requesting some person therein named to pay, or deliver money, goods, or other property to some other person specified, or to his order, or to the bearer, is called an Order. (See Chart.) Orders for money are generally known as Checks, or Drafts, or Bills of Exchange, as will be presently explained. "The person on whom an order may be given is under no legal obligation to pay it, unless he first engages to do so. Orders are generally considered payable on presentation, though they are sometimes *accepted* by the person on whom they are drawn, to be paid at *another* time. This may be done by his simply writing the word *"Accepted"* either across the back or face of the order, (but usually the latter, and in *red ink,*) and signing his name to it. Before this is done, an order may be regarded as evidence of debt, and as a claim upon the *drawer* of it; but afterwards it becomes a claim upon the *acceptor*, who in accepting agrees to pay."

Checks.

An ORDER addressed to a bank by a person who has money deposited in the bank, requesting the payment of money to the bearer, to a person named in the check, or to his order, is called a Check. "Checks are usually drawn and used in the place where both parties to them reside, and where the bank is located, and for convenience, are generally made payable to *bearer.* While a depositor has money to his credit at a bank, his checks are paid on presentation; but, when his credits are drawn out, his checks are no longer paid, unless by *special* arrangement. Checks are, therefore, generally presented to a bank for payment as soon after they are given as practicable, and usually, and very properly, within a day or two."

Drafts.

An ORDER addressed by one person, or by one bank, or mercantile house, to another, requesting the payment of *money* to a person named therein, to his order, or, *sometimes*, to the *bearer*, is called a Draft. " Checks which are drawn by a *depositor* upon a bank at home, and *handed* to the payee, are commonly made payable to the *bearer ;* but drafts, which are usually drawn by a bank in one place upon a bank in another place, and are generally sent to the payee *by mail*, from prudential reasons, are properly drawn payable to a person named, or to *his order.* Drafts made payable to a person named, or his order, will not be paid at the bank unless they bear the indorsement of the payee. When a draft is made payable at sight, or ten, or thirty days after sight, three additional days, known as ' days of grace,' are allowed for payment, by established usage in both Europe and America. Drafts are, therefore, sometimes drawn payable at sight, or at a specified time, ' without grace,' but, when drafts or bills are made payable on demand, or without any specified time, they are considered payable immediately on presentation, without allowing any days of grace.

"The person who makes, or draws and signs a draft, is called the *maker*, or *drawer*, of the draft ; the person to whom it is addressed, or upon whom the draft is made is called the *drawee*, and the person to whom, or to whose order it is made payable, is called the *payee.* In case the payee, by indorsement, transfers his right to the draft to another party, the latter party, or holder, is called the *indorsee.* Any person who rightfully possesses a draft is known as its *holder.*

When drafts are on time, or are made payable ten, twenty, or sixty days after sight, they should be presented by the holder to the drawee, or person on whom they are drawn, as soon as received, for acceptance. "In case the drawee accepts a draft, he writes the word 'accepted' either across its back or face, (usually the latter, and in red ink,) and dates and signs it. (See Accepted Draft.) The drawee then becomes the *acceptor*, and the time when the draft becomes due will be reckoned from the date of acceptance. A draft, *before* its acceptance, may be considered as an evidence of indebtedness by the drawer, or *maker* of it, to the *payee*," but, after its acceptance, a draft may be regarded as a promissory note, of which the *drawee*, or person on whom it is drawn, by his acceptance, becomes the maker, and the original maker becomes the indorser. If the acceptor fails to pay the draft when due, the original maker will be held responsible for its payment.

SPECIAL DIRECTIONS.—The teacher should call the attention of the class to the Forms of Drafts on the Charts, as follows : Commencing with the first, or Unaccepted Draft, he should show them that it is an Order, (See Definition); that it is drawn for money, by one person, upon another person, and is, hence, a Draft, (See Definition); that Curtis is the drawer, or *maker*, Munson the *drawee*, and Walworth the *payee;* that Munson must accept the draft before he is responsible

(8)

for its payment, when due ; that "*Acceptance*," in commercial *parlance*, means a "promise to pay ;" that he has so promised, showing the Form of Acceptance ; that it is drawn payable at ten days' sight ; that it was first seen and accepted by Munson, June 8th, 1871, and is, hence, due thirteen days thereafter, adding "three days of grace," which should be explained; that the draft, after acceptance, has the characteristics of a promissory note, Munson being the maker, and Curtis the indorser, etc. After which, the teacher should question the class upon all the points explained. In a similar manner, each Business Form on the Charts should be explained before the class are allowed to copy it.

Bills of Exchange.

DRAFTS and Bills of Exchange are essentially of the same import, and governed by the same laws, the principle difference being in the name. Drafts drawn by parties in one state, or country, upon persons in the same state or country, are sometimes called Bills of Domestic Exchange. If drawn by parties residing in different states or countries, or drawn in one country and made payable in another, they are called Bills of Foreign Exchange.

Sets of Exchange.

" A SET OF EXCHANGE embraces several Bills of Exchange, (usually three,) of the same date and tenor. When any of the Set is paid, the others are void. The object of a Set of Exchange is to provide beforehand against any inconvenience in case one of the Set should be lost in transmission. The holder of a Set of Exchange may send the First and Second of the Set forward for payment, under different dates, or by different conveyances, and retain the Third himself. Then, in case one is miscarried, the other may reach its destination and be paid. If both are lost, the Third may be used. Instead of First, Second, and Third, of Exchange, the different bills of a Set are sometimes known as Original, Duplicate, and Triplicate."

Receipts.

A WRITTEN statement, signed by the giver of it, acknowledging that he has received from another a specified amount of money, goods, or other property, is called a Receipt. It is *prima facie* evidence of the facts contained in it, but may be impeached by the party giving it.

Contracts.

An agreement between two or more parties for the doing, or not doing, of some specified thing, is called a Contract, The essential requisites of a good and valid contract are : First.—Parties able to contract ; for we cannot conceive of a contract without parties. Second.—A good and sufficient consideration, (unless the contract is under seal,) for this is, in legal contemplation, the cause of the contract ; but, if the consideration have some *real* value, however inadequate, it is sufficient. Third.—The consent of the contracting parties, without which, there is in law, no contract. Fourth.— A thing to be contracted for, or the subject matter of the contract.

Forms of Bills.

The teacher should see that the nature and use of the different Forms of Bills are thoroughly understood by the class. It is quite important that Bills of Goods, sold, or Services given, should be rendered to the party receiving them ; and they should be required by him. Especially should the buyer require a "Bill of Parcels" from the seller, not only that he may know the extent of his purchases, but also to protect him against error, or fraud, in the seller's account.

Rules for Interest.

THE different divisors for any rate per cent. given in the "Rules for Interest," may be found by dividing 360, (the number of interest days in a year, which custom has made legal,) by the rate per cent., dropping the cipher from 360, when the quotient will be a whole number without it; but when it will not, the cipher must be retained.

EXPLANATION.—In reckoning interest, we may multiply the principal by the rate per cent., to find the interest for one year, which we may divide by 360, to find the interest for one day; but, since the rate per cent. is a multiplier, we may cancel it with an equal factor in the divisor, 360. The remaining factor will be the divisor sought. Thus, dividing 360, (dropping the cipher, which avails nothing in multiplying or dividing,) by 4, (rate per cent.,) we obtain the quotient, 9, or the divisor given in the rule for this rate. The rate per cent. disappears, and, hence, the rule: "Multiply the principal by the time in days, and divide by 9." In like manner, we may obtain the divisor for any other rate per cent. given in "The Rules."

Letter-Writing.

EVERY individual in the community, who occupies any important station ; and, indeed, every person, high or low, rich or poor, may have, and, probably, will have, occasion to write letters. To do this in a neat and easy manner is of no trifling consequence ; and yet, every one who has ever looked at the letters in any post-office, must have observed the very general want of taste and neatness in the modes of folding and superscribing letters ; and, if the contents should be examined, they would be found to correspond with the external appearance.

"Now, it should be the aim of every teacher to impart instruction on the subject of letter-writing. General directions and explanations, in reference to the commencing and closing of a letter, the manner of folding, superscribing, and sealing, may be given to a whole school, by using the black-board,—in the absence of any better means,—and it will not require much of the teacher's time or attention, to furnish all the instruction that may be needed.

"It is to be hoped that more consideration may be attached to this simple, but useful exercise, and that all pupils may possess the ability, when they cease attending school, to write letters which shall be accurate and natural in their style, correct in orthography, systematic and proper in all their parts. A letter neatly written, correctly expressed, and properly folded and superscribed, will always prove a ' letter of recommendation ' to its writer; while the reverse will exert an influence in no respect favorable or complimentary."

General Directions.

THE teacher, with pointer in hand, may call the attention of the class to the Letter-Writing Chart, as follows :

TEACHER.—"Here we have the Arrangement of a Letter, showing : First.—The name of the place where it is written, and date of writing, as in the form below, thus, ' Detroit, Mich., Sept. 7, 1871.' Second.—The complimentary address, at the left, and one line below the name of place and date, thus, ' Messrs. Nichols & Hall.' Third.—The body of the letter, commencing at some distance from the left side, and one line below the complimentary address, thus, ' I arrived in this city,' etc. Fourth.—A new sentence, leaving a space between it, and the one preceding, thus, ' I have encouraging letters,' etc. Fifth.—New topic, commencing with indented line, thus, 'Please send me,' etc. Sixth.—Complimentary closing, one line below the body of the letter, and commencing near the middle of the line, thus, ' Yours, respectfully.' Seventh.—Signature, one line below the complimentary closing, and to the right, thus, ' James Henderson,' etc."

The attention of the class should be particularly called to the Forms of Letters Nos. 1 and 2, containing orders for goods; the first to be sent by express, the second by mail. The manner of superscribing the envelope, and the place for the stamp, should likewise receive due attention. It is requested by the Post-Office Department, at Washington, that the county be included in the superscription. When this is done, it should be written in the lower left-hand corner of the envelope. By the use of the Blank Letter Form, together with the black-board, if necessary, the teacher may give the class a great variety of "Complimentary addresses," and "Closings," and such other instruction, as may be necessary to a complete knowledge of this useful accomplishment.

Book-Keeping.

HERE is scarcely any situation in life, in which a knowledge of Book-Keeping may not be of much service. Its importance and general utility are such as to demand for it a more prominent place in our schools than it has, heretofore, received. It is a branch to which the attention of the older pupils, of *both sexes*, in all our schools, may be profitably given; for it not unfrequently happens that females have occasion for a practical use of knowledge thus acquired. But, if this should seldom or never be the case, the advantages of writing out a set of books, merely as a disciplinary exercise, would amply compensate for all time and attention devoted to it.   *   *   *

"A great amount of information may be imparted by an instructor without the aid of a regular text-book, though it would be preferable to use one. The nature and object of the day-book, ledger, cash-book, etc., should be fully and clearly explained, and everything in relation to each made as simple as possible. A little time

(9)

with the aid of black-board,—(in the absence of charts,)
—will enable the teacher to make everything sufficiently plain and clear."

Definitions.

BOOK-KEEPING.—Book-Keeping is the art of record-
ing business transactions in such a manner, as at any
time, to show the true state of one's pecuniary affairs.

DEBTOR AND CREDITOR.—Whenever one person buys
anything from another, which he does not pay for at the
time, he is said to go in debt for it, and is called a Debt-
or.

When a person sells anything without receiving his
pay at the time, he is said to give credit for it, and is
called a Creditor.   In keeping accounts it is customary
to write Dr. for Debtor, and Cr. for Creditor.

PERSONAL AND REAL ACCOUNTS.—Personal Accounts
are accounts kept with persons with whom we transact
business.

Real Accounts are accounts kept with realties ; and
include accounts of things which a person possesses.
Of this class are Cash, Merchandise, Field Accounts,
etc., etc.

TITLES OF ACCOUNTS.—The Title of an account is simply the name by which the account is known.   If we
have accounts with two persons of the same name, they

should be distinguished by giving the residence of each, or in some other effectual way.

General Directions.

1.—The teacher should prepare the Book-keeping Class for the study, by giving them, in advance, a brief, general view of the subject, or, at least, so much of it as is presented by these Charts. The nature and object of the Ledger, Day-Book, and Cash-Book, should be clearly explained, and, everything in relation to each, made as simple as possible, and such other information should be given as may be necessary to a good, general idea of the subject.

2.—Each member of the class should be provided with the requisite number of blank-books, for copying, or writing up the Forms given on the Charts. It would be well for the teacher to superintend the preparation of these books. The paper of which they should be made can generally be obtained, already ruled, at any book-store. Three books only will be necessary,—the Single Ledger, for the accounts requiring but one book, The Day-Book, and Day-Book Ledger. The paper for the Single Ledger and Day-Book, may be ruled alike; that for the Day-Book Ledger should be "Ledger Ruled." There is this difference between the Single and Day-Book Ledger,—the former requires two pages, or a folio, for an account, the Dr. entries are made upon the left page, and the Cr. entries upon the right page, while, in the latter, the Dr. and Cr. entries are both made upon the same page, thus requiring but one page for an account. The books having been prepared, the pupils should commence and copy, into their respective books, the Forms given on the Charts, constantly endeavoring to understand fully the reason for each entry. The teacher should anticipate any difficulty that is likely to arise, by stating the transactions, and showing how they are entered in the accounts, and why so entered. This may be done in the form of a question ; thus, for example :

TEACHER.—"If I sell A. E. Gage 65 bushels of Rye, at one dollar a bushel, how will I enter the transaction in his account ? Do I, by this transaction, owe him, or does he owe me ? Then, upon which side of the account shall I make the entry?" etc.

Questions like these may be given until the class thoroughly understand each entry they are required to copy.

3.—When the teacher becomes satisfied that this is the case, other books may be prepared and the class required to write up the examples given in this book. In so doing they should not be allowed to consult the Forms on the Charts. This having been satisfactorily accomplished, both in respect to neatness and accuracy, —which should be rigidly insisted upon,—

4.—The teacher may prepare short examples involving the different kinds and forms of accounts given on the Charts, and require the class to write up the same correctly ; or he may now encourage them to make a practical use of the knowledge already obtained, by opening up actual accounts with similar effects, at home.

The practice of keeping actual accounts in this way, While it familiarizes the mind with the forms of accounts, and affords a daily discipline not otherwise easily attainable, also presents the best possible opportunity for learning the details, and hence stimulating an interest in whatever business the account is kept with.

Preparatory Instruction.

HAVING placed the Book-Keeping Chart upon the wall, the teacher, with pointer in hand, may say :

TEACHER.—" Class, I wish to show you what a simple thing it is to keep accounts ; and to illustrate this let us suppose that I am having deal with A. E. Gage, a country merchant. I buy of him from time to time without paying for what I buy, and sell to him in like manner, without being paid for what I sell. Hence, we "run in debt to each other." Now, I wish to have an account of all our transactions, so that I may know at any time how our business affairs stand. So, if you please,

I will engage you to keep this account for me. You will first write his name above the account, as you see here, (pointing,) to show with whom it is kept. I will then give you the items of the account, and you may enter all that he owes me upon this, the left side of the account, and all that I owe him upon this, the right side of the account. This, (pointing to the left side,) we will call the Debtor side, (explain why,) and write Dr. for Debtor ; and this, we will call the Creditor side, and write Cr. for Creditor.

" You see how simple this is, and how easy, by adding up each side, and finding the difference between them, to discover which one is *really* indebted to the other upon settlement, and how much, (perform the work,) and this is the *principal object* of keeping accounts.

" Now, for fear that some of you may forget what I have said, let me repeat ;—all there is absolutely essential to the keeping of any account is, first, the title of the account, to show with whom or what the account is kept, (for accounts are sometimes kept with things, as well as with persons,) and secondly, two sides to the account, the left for the Dr. and the right for the Cr. entries.

" All accounts whatever may be kept in this simple form, and, indeed, some merchants do keep their accounts with all persons with whom they deal, in this way, devoting a folio, or two pages, to each one's account. This is called the Ledger form, and the book in which they are kept is called the Ledger.

Accounts kept in this form require but one book, and since they demand less writing than when kept in any other way, would doubtless never be kept otherwise, were it not for the inconvenience of turning from page to page throughout a book of several hundred pages, to find a person's account, whenever entries have to be made, as is often the case in a large business, to the accounts of hundreds, or even thousands of persons daily. In such cases it is much more convenient to enter the transactions of the day, at the time and in the order of their occurrence, all upon the same or successive pages, if more than one is required. But while entries to a number of different accounts are more readily made by the use of this form, the accounts are intermingled, and scattered throughout the entire book, and those belonging to the same person, or title, require to be brought together on folios, or pages, by themselves, in order to determine the condition of the several accounts kept.

" This is accomplished by the use of a Ledger, in which, is opened, *one* account with each person having items of account in the Day-Book, and, into this Ledger account, all the scattered items of the same account in the Day-Book are carried. The process of gathering the separate items of one's account from the Day-Book, and carrying them into the Ledger, under one name, or title, is called Posting.

" An account will stand in the Ledger, after posting from the Day-Book, just as if it had been entered in the Ledger in the first place. Thus, you see, the Ledger form is the only one absolutely necessary, and the Day-Book is used as a sort of memorandum, to catch and hold the accounts until they can be entered in the Ledger.

" This is all I will tell you to-day; but, from time to time, as it may seem necessary, I will tell you something more of the different kinds of accounts, and of the details of keeping them, of which I have purposely omitted to speak at this exercise. I will now give you the items of my account with A. E. Gage, after which you may copy the account into your books, from the Chart."

Closing a Personal Account.

TEACHER.—(*Placing A. E. Gage's Account before the class.*)—" Class, before an account can be properly closed, its Dr. and Cr. sides must balance. This will, of course, always be the case when the account is settled; but, if it is an unsettled account, and it is desirable to close it for any purpose whatever, then the account may be balanced by making, upon the smaller side, a fictitious entry of the difference between the two sides. This is called the ' Balance Entry,' and is made upon the supposition that the amount entered has actually been received, or paid by us, (as it may appear from the side upon which the entry is made,) and the account settled. But, since this is not the fact, and the amount of this Balance Entry is still unpaid, as in this account with A. E. Gage, we open a new account, and charge or debit him with this amount. We may open his account upon the same page, as we see here, or upon some other page of the same book, or in some other book, as we please. But before this new account is opened, we should finally close the old one. This we do, after having made the Balance Entry, by drawing single lines under the money columns, and, after adding them, and placing the amount under each, we draw double lines, to show that the account is balanced and closed. The Balance Entry and the rulings are usually made in red ink."

The Cash Account.

TEACHER.—(Placing the Cash Account before the class.)—" An account may be kept with Cash on the same principle as with persons. If we perform labor for Cash, or sell property for Cash, it is manifest Cash is Dr., just as a person would be in case we should labor for *him,* or sell property to him on account. So, if we buy Sugar, and pay for it in Cash, as in this example,

---

*From " Mayhew's University Book-Keeping,"—an excellent work.

(10)

(*Pointing to the Cash Account on the Chart,*) we should make Cash Cr., just as we should make a person Cr., were we to buy of him on account. Cash now does something for us ; it is the giver to us of the sugar, and is, hence, Cr.

" The reason for making the Dr. and Cr. entries as above stated, may, perhaps, be better understood by supposing a person keeps his money in a drawer, whose name is Cash. On opening the account we put what money we have into the drawer, and debit Cash, which is the receiver.

" The first entry to the Cash account, it is apparent, must be on the Dr. side ; for we must put money into the drawer before we can take it out; or, in other words, we must receive Cash before we can pay it out.

" Whenever the drawer is the receiver of money, Cash is Dr. ; and whenever the drawer is the giver of money, Cash is Cr. for the sum taken from it."

" But, for present purposes, it is entirely unneccessary to take this philosophical view of the matter. All that is required in keeping this account correctly, is to enter all Cash on hand when the account is opened, and all subsequent Cash receipts upon the left, or Dr. side of the account, and all Cash paid out upon the right, or Cr. side of the account. The principal object in keeping a Cash account is to show the Cash on hand whenever desirable. This is done by subtracting the amount paid out, (or the Cr. side,) from the amount received, (or the Dr. side of the account ;) for it is evident that the excess over what has been paid out must still be on hand. In business, this is usually done once a day, and the account balanced and closed, and a new account opened, (upon the same page if there is room,) for the purpose of showing, in a *single entry*, the Cash on hand."

Closing the Cash Account.

TEACHER.—"The manner of closing this account, is similar to that of closing a personal account. After finding the difference between the two sides, or the ' Balance of Cash ' on hand, the amount is entered upon the Cr. side, upon the supposition that it has actually been paid out. But since this is not the case, we open another account with Cash and Dr. it, for this amount, still on hand. The ruling is the same as for the closing of a personal account.

Cornfield Account.

TEACHER.—(*Placing the Cornfield Account before the class.*)—" Class, accounts may be kept with a Cornfield, or with any branch of one's business, just as

with persons.   Whenever we give anything to the field,
or incur any expense on its account, it is made Dr.;
and whenever we receive anything from the field, whether in money from sales to others, or for our own use, the
proper entry is made upon the Cr. side of the account.

"In this account, the footings of the Dr. entries,
show that we have paid out $142.25, on account of the
field.   The footings of the Cr. side, show that we have
received $487.84 from the field.   By subtraction, it ap-
pears we have received $345.59 more from the field
than we have paid on its account.   This is the amount
of our *net gain.*   If we wish to balance the account,
we enter this amount upon the smaller, or Dr. side of
the account, upon the supposition that it has been paid
out for the field ; but, since this is not the case, and to
show that the entry indicates a *net gain*, it should be
made in red ink.   Accounts whose Balance Entry show
a gain or loss, unlike the cash or personal accounts,
need not necessarily be opened again.

" By keeping accounts in this way with a cornfield,
with a wheat field, with a potato field, with sheep and
wool, or with the different branches of one's business,
whatever it may be, persons may determine, with great
accuracy, what pursuits afford certain profits, and what
particular departments of their business are most lucra-
tive ; and by regulating their business accordingly, they
can best promote their own interests, and, at the same
time, contribute the most effectually to the prosperity
of the community in which they live."

The Day-Book.

TEACHER.—(*Placing the Day-Book Chart before the class.*)—" Class, I will now give you a brief description of the Day-Book. It is ruled with a space here at the left, (pointing,) for entering the page of the Ledger to which the account is posted. All of the accounts upon this page, as you see by the figure 1, are posted to the first page of the Ledger. Then a broad space, as you see here, (pointing,) is appropriated for the title of the account, with a description of the articles bought or sold, at the right of which, (pointing,) are two sets of money columns. When several items are entered to the account of the same person at one time, as we see here in Henry Wright's account, Jan. 2, it is best to enter the amount of each item in the first set of money columns, as follows : (pointing to the amounts 5 and 1.80,) and, after adding them, carry the whole amount into the second set of money columns, preparatory to posting. The date in the Day-Book is written at the head of each page, as you see here, (pointing to Monday, Jan. 1, 1872,) and if changed upon a page is entered in the middle of the broad space, as you see here, (pointing to Jan. 2 and 3,) instead of at the left. Dr. and Cr. entries are sometimes indicated in the Day-Book by writing Dr. or Cr., as the case may be, in the middle of the broad space, as you see here, in Chas. Culver's account of Jan. 1. Dr. and Cr. entries may also be indicated by the words

" To," and " By," without writing Dr. or Cr., as in this credit entry, " By Cash," (pointing,) in Henry Wright's account of Jan. 2. When entries are made in this form, " To," denotes a Dr. entry, and " By," a Cr. entry.

The Ledger.

TEACHER.—(*Placing the Ledger before the class.*)— " Class, the Ledger is a book to which the entries of the Day-Book are transferred, in a condensed form, and so arranged as to present the account of each person on a page by itself, as you see here, (pointing to Henry Wright's account.) The ruling of the Ledger is as follows :—Each page is divided by double perpendicular lines, into two equal parts, the left, (pointing,) being for Dr. entries, and the right for Cr. entries. Each side is ruled like the Single Ledger, before spoken of, with the addition of a space at the left of the money columns, on each side, as you see here, (pointing,) in which is entered the page of the Day-Book, from which the entry is posted. The entries in these three accounts are all posted from the 1st page of the Day-Book, as we see by the figure 1, in this space, before each amount entered. Being preceded by a Day-Book, to which reference may be made for particulars, the accounts in the Ledger will often occupy much less space than in any other form; as you see here in the entries " To Mdse." " To Sundries," " By Cash," etc., etc. This economy of space is obtained by carrying *amounts* only to the Ledger, and *omitting details* which appear in the Day-Book, and to which reference may readily be made when necessary."

Posting.

TEACHER.—(*Placing Day-Book and Ledger Charts before the class.*)—" Class, I have previously told you that the process of gathering the scattered items of one's account from the Day-Book, and carrying them into the Ledger, under one name, or title, is called Posting. Now, let us open an account in the Ledger with Henry Wright, whose name we find in the Day-Book, and see if we cannot gather the scattered items of account with him, in the Day-Book, and carry them all correctly into this *one* account with him, in the Ledger. We find here, upon the Day-Book, of Jan. 1, (*pointing,*) that Henry Wright is Dr. ' To balance of old Account, $62.' Now, since he is Dr. here, we will carry the entry to the Dr. side of his account in the Ledger, and make the entry as follows: 'Jan. 1, (same date as in the Day-Book,) To Balance of old Account, 1 page of the Day-Book, $62.' Now since this account is upon the 1st page of the Ledger, we go back to the Day-Book, and make a figure 1 here in this space at the left, to show the Ledger page, and also that the entry has been posted.

We find next in the Day Book of Jan. 2, Henry Wright, Dr., to butter and sugar, the whole amount of which is $6,80, which we carry to the Dr. side of the Ledger, in the same manner. But we find also, that he is Cr. by Cash, $25, in this same transaction; and since he is Cr. here, we carry this entry to the Cr. side of his account in the Ledger, as follows: 'Jan. 2, By Cash, 1 page Day-Book, $25' (pointing), and making a figure 1 in the Day-Book, to show the Ledger page, and also that it is posted. We next find in the Day-Book of Jan. 3, Henry Wright, Cr., 'By C. A. Reed's note for $30,' which we carry to the Cr. side, as above, etc., etc.

Example I.

This example consists of a series of transactions between the teacher, for whom the student is book-keeper, and A. E. Gage, a country merchant.

TRANSACTION 1.—*May* 1, 1872.—I sell A. E. Gage 65 bushels of Rye, at $1 a bushel.

As in this transaction, Gage is the receiver, and he does not now pay me for the Rye, the entry belongs upon the Dr. side of the account, and is made as follows: (See Chart.)

TRANSACTION 2.—*May* 4.—I buy of A. E. Gage, 1 Single Carriage for $135.

Here Gage is the giver, and, as I do not now pay

him for the carriage, the entry belongs upon the Cr. side of the account.

Transaction 3.—*May* 9.—I sell A. E. Gage, 1 Ton of Hay for $17.

Here Gage is the receiver, and hence the entry belongs on the Dr. side of his account.

Transaction 4.—*May* 13.—I buy of A. E. Gage, G. Lemon's order on Fred Cole for $22.

Here Gage is the giver, and is hence Cr. (See Chart.)

Transaction 5.—*May* 20.—I have done A. E. Gage 5 days' work with team, at $2 a day.

Gage is here Dr. for services rendered.

Transaction 6.—*May* 25.—I buy of A. E. Gage 25 lbs. of Pork at 10 cents a pound.

Gage is again the giver, and is hence Cr.

Transaction 7.—*May* 27.—Paid A. E. Gage $80 in cash.

Here Gage is the receiver, and is hence Dr.

Transaction 8.—*May* 29.—I buy of A. E. Gage 6 doz. Eggs t 20 cents a dozen, for which I give him Cr.

Example II.

This example exhibits an account with Cash. All Cash received is entered upon the Dr. side, and all Cash paid out, is entered upon the Cr. side of the account.

January 1.—1872.—I find upon counting my Cash that I have $123.41.

(11)

TRANSACTION 1.—*Jan.* 3.—I buy 24 ℔s. of Tea at $1 a pound, for which I pay Cash.

TRANSACTION 2.—*Jan.* 5.—I sell 25 bushels of oats at 40 cents a bushel, for which I receive Cash.

TRANSACTION 3.—*Jan.* 12.—I pay A. Roy $80 in Cash.

TRANSACTION 4.—*Jan.* 16.—I sell for Cash 4 tons of hay at $20 a ton.

JANUARY 31.—I have this day closed my Cash account, to find the balance on hand. How much is it? Upon what side of the account do I make my balance entry, and what shall next be done with it?

Example III.

This example exhibits an account with a Cornfield of 10 acres, The field is charged with every item of expense incurred in raising, harvesting, and marketing the crop, and credited at marketable rates for all it returns.

TRANSACTION 1.—*May* 1, 1872.—I have done 7 days' plowing with horse team, in my Cornfield, which is worth $4 a day.

TRANSACTION 2.—*May* 9.—I have done 2 days' harrowing, worth $2 a day.

TRANSACTION 3.—*May* 11.—I have done 1 days' work marking out the ground, which is worth $2.

TRANSACTION 4.—*May* 13.—I have used in planting, 1¼ bushels seed corn, worth $1 a bushel.

TRANSACTION 5.—*May* 13.—The planting has required 5 days' work, worth $1,25 a day.

TRANSACTION 6.—*Nov.* 18.—I sell 700 bushels of corn, at 60 cents a bushel.

TRANSACTION 7.—*Nov.* 24.—I have kept for use 100 bushels of corn, worth 60 cents a bushel.

TRANSACTION 8.—*Nov.* 25.—The "Balance of Expenses" incurred in cultivating, hoeing, harvesting, marketing the crop, and the interest on the land, for one year at $80 per acre, amounts to $100.75, which I make here in one entry, from the total footings of the same in my pocket memorandum.

TRANSACTION 9.—*Nov.* 30.—I sell 8 loads of Stalks, at 98 cents a load. The balance of the Stalks were swept away by a sudden freshet, and no account has been made of them, although I should have given the field credit for them, since the loss is mine, and not the field's.

What entry must be made on the Dr. side of the account, in closing it, as the profit on this field of corn ?

Example IV.—Day-Book.

This example consists of a series of transactions between the teacher, who is supposed to be a merchant, and certain customers of his

INVENTORY OF MY ASSETTS.

Monday, January 1, 1872.

Henry Wright owes me on account $62.

I owe as follows :

George Mann on account $37.

TRANSACTION 1.—I have sold Charles Culver on account, 7 yds. Eng. Broadcloth, @ $5.00.

TRANSACTION 2.—I have bought of Charles Culver on account, 1 Ton of Hay, @ $20.

Tuesday, January 2, 1872.

TRANSACTION 3.—I have sold Henry Wright on account,

10 ℔s. Butter, @ 50 c.

15 " Brown Sugar, @ 12 c.

He pays $25 in cash on account.

Wednesday, January 3, 1872.

TRANSACTION 4.—I have sold George Mann 12 yds. Blk. Silk, @ $2—have paid him $13 in cash, which settles our account.

TRANSACTION 5.—I have sold Charles Culver on account, 50 lbs. Crushed Sugar, @ 20 c.—Received of him $25 in cash.

TRANSACTION 6.—I have bought of Henry Wright C. A. Reed's note, for $30.

Phonography.

PHONOGRAPHY is a system of short-hand, based upon the plan of spelling words, strictly by sound. To do this, it is necessary to have more letters, or signs, than there are in the ordinary alphabet. Thus, while the latter contains twenty-six letters, Phonography has forty, or a letter for each sound, in the English language.

In presenting the phonographic alphabet upon the Chart, the Consonants have been arranged by themselves, and the Vowels by themselves.

Consonants.

The Consonant signs number twenty-four and are as follows :—(See Chart.) P, B, T, D, CH, J, K, G, F, V, TH, TH, S, Z, SH, ZH, M, N, NG, H, L, R, (made two ways,) W and Y. It will be observed that corresponding sounds, are represented by corresponding signs, the difference in the sounds being indicated by shading the sign for the heavier, or sub-vocal sound.

The new Consonant letters in the phonographic alphabet are CH, as heard in the words *chew* or *each*; TH, as in *thigh* or *oath*; TH, as in *thy* or *soothe*; SH, as in *she* or *ash*; ZH, as in *azure* or *measure*; NG, as in *ink* or *lung*. The phonographic letter G, is used only for the consonant sound, heard in the word *go* or *egg*. The consonant sound in such words as *gee* and *age*, being represented by the Phonographic J.

Vowels.

THE phonographic Vowel-signs, of which there are sixteen, including four double vowels, or diphthongs, consist of dots, dashes, etc., placed to the consonant stem in three positions, viz: At the *beginning*, *middle* and *end*. The consonant-stem is of course no part of the vowel-sign. In the table of vowels, these signs and their positions, are shown by writing them near the consonant stem, *tee*. Thus, a heavy first place dot represents the vowel sound, (*a*)h, (not a); second place, (*a*)te; third place, (*e*)at. A light first place dot represents the vowel-sound (*a*)t, (pronounce *at*, omitting the *t*); second place, (*e*)t; third place, (*i*)t. A heavy first place dash represents the vowel sound, (*a*)we; second place, (*o*)we; third place, (*oo*)ze (not double o). A light first place dash represents the vowel sound, (*o*)t ; second place, (*u*)t ; third place, f(*oo*)t, etc., etc.

General Directions.

READING.—The first thing to be done by the beginner, is to learn the new alphabet, so that when he sees a sign, he will immediately know what sound it stands for ; and when he hears a sound, he will as readily write its sign.

In the Chart of Phonographic Words, the key to each word will be found directly under it, and the pupil should carefully study every word, making reference to the table of consonants and vowels, to ascertain why it is written as here indicated. By being very thorough just here, not only will a good knowledge be acquired of the principles of phonographic spelling, but the new signs will be pretty well fixed in the memory. Repeat it over and over again.

WRITING.—In writing a word phonographically, the consonant signs are always written first, and the vowel afterwards placed to them. " When a vowel occurs before a consonant, the vowel sign is written to the *left* of the consonant sign, if it be perpendicular or inclined, and above, if it be horizontal ; when a vowel comes after the consonant, the vowel sign is written to the right of the consonant sign, if it be perpendicular or inclined, and below if it be horizontal."

ORTHOGRAPHY.—The Study of Phonography is also one of the best methods of acquiring a knowledge of Orthography. It tends to make one critical in the analysis of every word, and perfect in pronunciation. As a special concert drill, the teacher may call the attention of the class to the Chart of "Words in Munson's Phonography," and after showing them that each word is composed of but two sounds, and hence should have but two letters to correspond, he may require them to pronounce, first, the word in the ordinary spelling, and then the phonographic word, after having first spelled it by sound as follows: b—a bay, etc., etc.

.